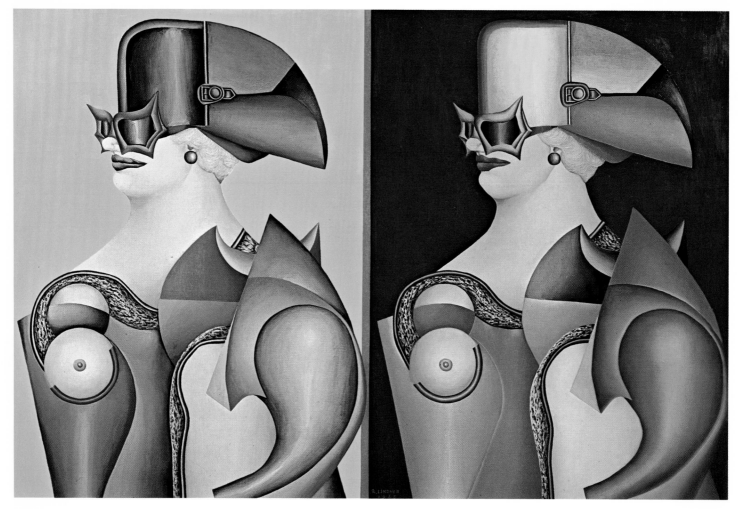

Richard Lindner. Double Portrait.   1965. Oil on canvas. 40 x 60. Lent by Miss Helen Mary Harding

Human Concern/Personal Torment The Grotesque in American Art

by Robert Doty Curator, Whitney Museum of American Art

Whitney Museum of American Art   New York

Whitney Museum of American Art, New York
October 14—November 30, 1969

University Art Museum, University of California, Berkeley
January 20—March 1, 1970

Acknowledgments

For encouragement, advice and assistance, I am pleased to thank Jan von Adlmann, Donald Baum, Sylvan Cole, Arne Ekstrom, Mrs. Bella Fishko, Miss Suzanne Foley, Allan Frumkin, Walter Hopps, Ivan Karp, Philip Linhares, Mrs. Dorothy Norman, Alfonso Ossorio, Joseph Raffael, Mel Ramos, Peter Selz, Allan Stone, and Miss Nancy Stout. Many colleagues will have contributed assistance by the time the exhibition and catalogue are completed. I especially want to thank John I. H. Baur for his support and consultation. Stephen Weil made many suggestions and assisted with allied projects. Miss Emily Shields and Miss Gail Lloyd helped to prepare the catalogue. Mrs. Jane Margulies has provided expert assistance in many ways throughout the course of the project. Special assistance in the production of the catalogue has been provided by Cordier & Ekstrom, Inc.; Mrs. Bella Fishko; Reese Palley; Allan Stone; Time, Inc.; Mrs. Eleanor Ward.

The Whitney Museum of American Art is grateful to those collectors, galleries and institutions which have lent works to the exhibition. Above all we are indebted to the artists, who have devoted their lives to enriching our own.

The frame of reference for man has been the myths of his existence. In this modern age the dominant myths have been rationalism, the worth of the individual and the superiority of technology. But these myths are disintegrating, constantly losing validity in the face of man's actions and preferences. The constant state of war, a rising crime rate and the continual desire for violence in entertainment testify to their fallibility. Matthew Brady could not sell his photographs of the Civil War battlefields to a public tired of carnage. But only three years after the Second World War, the film *Battleground* appeared in American theatres. Writers and film-makers invested the gangster and gunfighter with heroic qualities of lengendary magnitude. Television and press insure that the vision of violent death is constantly available to everyone. The camera is irrefutable witness to the outrages of mankind and its veracity stimulates a basic lust for the outrageous.

The artist as commentator, and analyst, reflects the strength or weakness of the dominant myths. "An artist cannot influence what will happen in society, he can only observe and comment on its past...His paintings are his emotional responses...to history as it happened to him,"[1] said Ed Paschke, and presents in his paintings a procession of brutish entertainment personalities and events, including a presidential assassin and the war in Vietnam.

Ed Kienholz created works entitled *The Illegal Operation, The Psycho-Vendetta Case* and *History As a Planter* because "the times dictate what the art will be..."[2] Goya's *Disasters of War,* 1812-20, Daumier's *Rue Transnonain,* 1834, and Picasso's *Guernica,* 1937, bear him out. Great responses to the transgressions of military power, eloquent testimony to the necessity of questioning the justification of man's existence, and damning evidence against the myth of rationality. So long as men of conscience are moved to create art, they will testify to the cracks in the myths of their time and to man's inherent vulnerability.

In 1854, Henry David Thoreau remarked that "The mass of men lead lives of quiet desperation." In 1969, the *Wall Street Journal* reported on a housing development in Maryland, of which the chief features were to be "armed guards standing watch day and night over a fenced-in compound. Hidden electronic sensors to foil intruders. Tight identity checks of all who seek to enter." Quite plainly there is reason for human concern over

Seymour Rosofsky. The Good Burghers of Lunidam (Number 7).
1968. Lithograph. 24 x 32. Lent by Phyllis Kind Gallery,
Chicago

the changing condition of mankind. Evil and tragedy have always been present in the affairs of man, and those whose lives remain untouched by its manifestations are rare. To those artists who are engaged not only in wresting signs and symbols from the chaos of action, but also in mocking the complacency, coarseness and banality of the environment, the contamination of life is the core of existence. For artists of this conviction, the world is estranged, life is absurd, the grotesque is the measure of all things, spiritual or material.

The grotesque is a form of art, with certain common characteristics. First, the rejection of reason, its benefits, protection and institutions. Second, immersion in the subconscious and its offspring, such as fear, passion and perversity, which often elicits a strong interest in sex and violence and not infrequently a commingling of the two. Third, a clash of elements, an obsession with opposites which force the co-existence of the beautiful with the repulsive, the sublime with the gross, humor with horror, the organic with the mechanical. Fourth, emphasis on ridicule, surprise and virulence, through caricature, the deformation and distortion of salient characteristics. The grotesque threatens the foundations of existence through the subversion of order and the treacherous reversal of familiar and hostile. Its value and vitality stem from the aberrations of human relationships and acts and therefore from man and his foibles, weakness and irresistible attractions. It is a direct and forceful means of exposing man to man, and man to himself.

"If it had not been for these things I might have lived out my life talking at street corners to scorning men. I might have to die, unmarked, unknown, a failure. Now we are not a failure. This is our career and our triumph. Never in our full life could we hope to do for tolerance, for justice, for man's understanding of man, as now we do by accident. Our words, our lives, our pains—nothing! The taking of our lives—lives of a good shoemaker and a poor fishpeddler—all! That moment belongs to us—that agony is our triumph."[3] Thus the condemned anarchist Bartolomeo Vanzetti addressed the court which had convicted him of murder. Many artists struggle for the triumph Vanzetti gained by accident, endeavoring to make their objects and images relevant to the needs of others. They assault the indifference of human relations, reveal man's inhumanity to man and the infamy of all mankind. They see the subversion of normal life, and fear the dissolution of the familiar world. They feel the frustration of helplessness and futility before ominous, sinister and malicious powers they were powerless to turn aside. They have experienced war, pestilence and personal turmoil. Their art absorbed their fears, anxiety and anger, and became monstrous. The subject matter and media may vary, but ridicule, absurdity, futility, terror, horror, distortion and repulsion are the elements from which their art is made. It is an art which deals with estrangement and the intensity of common experience, drawing upon the darker aspects of the human condition and the vile passions. The artist sees life as continuous torment, preferring the truth to hypocrisy and agreeing with Camus that "death alone awakens our feelings." From the ancient civilizations, through Bosch and Bruegel, to Goya and modern times, the artist has been both compelled and fascinated by the grotesque and its affinity for mankind.

For many artists, alienation is inevitable. "The cracked world around me impinges at every open sluice; and my very air is charged with waves and echoes and rays from a society and civilization in which I feel like a mixture of outlaw, leper and pariah."[4] Leonard Baskin's words echo his images. His portrait of the *Poet Laureate* is a summation of the human proclivity for hypocrisy and sham. Rico Lebrun felt an inexorable need to review the horror of the German concentration camps because "...they said I could draw as a bird sings. Possibly I still can. But there came a time when the image of man was so defaced that bird songs did not seem enough. If I had to lose all my virtues as a passable draftsman for the sake of speaking truly about the unmanageable design of our condition, I would do so gladly. Talent is one thing: life another."[5] For these, and many artists, the revelation of human failings is a necessity, the documentation of the forces of evil a duty and responsibility. Peter Saul paints with the tawdry colors so beloved by merchandisers, utilizes such ubiquitous symbols as the Coke bottle and dollar sign, draws biomorphic shapes which evoke visceral associations. His subjects are greed, lust, power, because they are life-forces and he is determined to "show people that what they want most to look at is not the kind of thing

Ed Paschke. Dos Criados.
1968. Oil on canvas. 48 x 40. Lent by the artist

that they will enjoy seeing."[6] The artist does not revel in the bizarre, neither does he lampoon for the sake of the idle jest nor try to titillate a jaded public. Rather he desperately seeks to engage the mind and spirit of the spectator, to bring him to a state of awareness that will permit no evasion. He forces the spectator to re-examine values, but he does not reject society. He feels alienated, but he does not relinquish hope. His work may be commentary, indictment, or denunciation, but on whatever level he chooses to act, he grapples with the real issues of mankind, knowing that art is more than embellishment and that he can make visual man's follies and estrangement.

Throughout the last century of American art, the artist has used the grotesque as a cudgel against politics and politicians, power and predators. Corruption and degradation prompted Thomas Nast to create images of evil. Through caricature, with its distortion of ugly reality and mockery, he made travesties of politicians, statesmen and the clergy. The images from his pen provoked laughter, disgust, and eventually, reform. The painters of the Ashcan School dealt with reality for the sake of reality, but George Bellows produced lithographs which castigated the suffering and unspeakable horror of the First World War. During the period between the wars, Charles Burchfield censured modern industrialism and its by-products, poverty, drabness, spiritual repression and destruction of natural resources. One of the first artists to sense the force of " the gathering storm" in Europe was David Smith. Courageously sweeping aside the constructivist concepts, wit and lyric sense which stimulated his work, Smith created a series of fifteen bronze plaques in 1937-40, entitled *Medals for Dishonor.* A scathing indictment of the crimes committed in the name of national destiny, the imagery of the plaques, a seething mass of figures and objects endowed with symbolic content, represents an ancestry of terror and the instruments of death unmistakably controlled by human hands. The first monumental, visual anti-war art in America, the *Medals for Dishonor* may now be seen as part of a continuing effort on the part of many artists to arouse a complacent public to the disasters of war. George Grosz saw the growing power of the Nazi terror and went on to chronicle the devastation of the Second World War. The dichotomy

David Smith. Medals for Dishonor: The Fourth Estate.
1939-40. Bronze. 8⅝ x 10½. Lent by The Estate of David
Smith, courtesy of Marlborough-Gerson Gallery

Paul Cadmus. Coney Island.
1935. Oil on canvas. 32¾ x 36¼ . Lent by Peter A. Paanakker
and the Los Angeles County Museum of Art

of affluence in America and terror in Southeast Asia produced a situation in which America was indifferent to the atrocities being committed in its name. The irony of the situation was not lost on Peter Saul, Wally Hedrick, Duane Hanson and Sigmund Abeles who excoriated corruption and savagery in Vietnam. By the repulsive, brutish nature of their images they defy fashion and simplistic approaches to concentrate on the grotesque, forcing their art to express the barbarity of man's actions.

A sense of duty continues to sustain the humanist art of our time. It has forced Theodore Roszak, like David Smith, to renounce the assurance of Constructivist principles for the uncertainties of the grotesque because, said Roszak, "the world is fundamentally and seriously disquieted and it is difficult to remain unmoved and complacent in its midst."[7] Such artists are no longer concerned with vague theories of "social realism," but rather dedicated to communicating directly their intense contempt, disillusionment and disgust for a political and social structure which continually permits, if not actually encourages, conflict and suffering. They are concerned with concepts such as guilt, atonement, and individual responsibility, while recognizing that the only values esteemed by the public are power and amusement. Robert Crumb, Spain and S. Clay Wilson, working in the style of the comic book, make succinct commentary on the coalescence of these values. In 1874, Thomas Nast directed his scorn toward the self-inflicted blindness of police power, and today a young cartoonist, Spain, is compelled to decry the vicarious lust and fascination of the public for legal brutality. One hundred years separate *Jewels Among Swine* and *Manning,* but the omnipresent threat of mis-used power makes one as modern as the other.

When John Singleton Copley tired of painting elegant portraits of elegant people, he turned to violence as his subject. *Watson and the Shark* is an image of high melodrama, a celebration of agony and the threat of death, man saved from the jaws of the monster. Violence for the sake of violence was not a staple of the artist in nineteenth century America but there were a few grand exceptions. Henry T. Tuckerman, writing on the life of Charles Deas, reported that "... his talent, even when manifest in the vagaries of a diseased mind, was often effective; one of his wild pictures, representing a black sea, over which a figure hung, suspended by a ring, while from the waves a monster was springing, was so horrible, that a sensitive artist fainted at the sight."[8] The French Revolution and its reign of terror inspired the artist to treat horror and death with high moral purpose. But the slaughter of the First World War banished any persisting desire to embellish the act or thought of death with the trappings of beauty or sentiment. When violence appeared in art during the 1930's, it was cloaked in the guise of social protest, such as *To the Lynching* by Paul Cadmus, or in the venomous faces of the bathers at *Coney Island*. The Second World War and the interminable conflict that followed, has insured that violence will continue to preoccupy the artist. Some have been touched directly by it. Lucas Samaras recalls "the bombings, the hiding, my aunt's ripped belly, the sound of executions, the strange pride in being visited by a catastrophe."[9] In the light of such experience, Samaras' work is both autobiographical and a metaphor of dread. The hideously transformed remnants of *Medusa* and *Child* by Bruce Conner express his concern for the imminent possibility of world annihilation and the power of strategists who have coined phrases such as "overkill," "balance of terror," and "megacorpse." Recently, civil strife has become a part of art, as well as life, in America. Duane Hanson employs the verisimilitude of the tableau to present the ugly brutality of the hatred between black and white, while David Freed graphically depicts the impenetrable barriers of the white neighborhood. So long as violence continues to be a facet of contemporary life, it will also be a significant subject for the artist.

The Greeks fashioned their gods and goddesses in perfected versions of their own bodies, thus unifying deity and man. But Christianity looked askance at the nude and the medieval artist treated the human body as an object of shame and derision. The modern artist has increasingly regarded the body as a receptacle of depravity and the victim of organic and spiritual forces, such as birth and death, which, in the work of Cosmo Campoli, Alfonso Ossorio and Ivan Albright, have assumed a corporal form. The inadequacy of man is expressed through the ugliness of his flesh. The body as the measure of man and beauty is ridiculed by Jim Nutt and Karl Wirsum. Instead of familiar contours and smooth flesh, Peter Saul and Jerry Savage offer the viscera as the true components of the human condition, while Ivan Albright, Leonard Baskin and Bruce Conner view it

Lucas Samaras. Untitled Sculpture.
1962. Mixed media. 5½ x 11⅜ x 8⅞ . Lent by Philip Johnson

Bruce Conner. Medusa.
1960. Mixed media. 10¾ x 11 x 22¼ . Collection of the
Whitney Museum of American Art, New York. Gift of Howard
and Jean Lipman Foundation, Inc.

as a vehicle of inevitable defilement. The grotesque takes the most familiar and intimate object, the human body, and re-forms it as a vulgar and ugly prison, strengthening the fears of decay and disease which are so carefully suppressed.

The physical world of man has been re-examined by artists who view object and environment as malevolent. Transformations took place as the artist attempted the forced coupling of ordinary objects of singular incompatibility. Federico Castellon and Eugene Berman stimulate repulsion for human identity by charging the body with repulsive or disturbing characteristics. Unexpected, arbitrary associations were an essential element of Surrealism, which opened new explorations in the substratum of the human soul. New impetus for the re-structuring of the object arrived with the discovery of junk. The debris of life was found to have redeeming social value. Indeed, in the hands of Robert Mallary, refuse was transfigured. Old tuxedos, impregnated with polyesters to give them permanence, became "tragic icons that are vestiges of doomed souls."[10] In California, which nurtured a distinguished group of assemblagists, including Ed Kienholz, junk constructions were the result of an abundant source of raw material and a cheerfully determined need to comment on waste and affluence. Another California product was Funk, an object-oriented, highly personal means of expression. Its practitioners make no moral judgments, offer no solutions for man's trouble, simply claw at his soft under-belly. Harold Paris, describes Funk as "organic, usually biomorphic, nostalgic, anthromorphic, sexual, glandular, visceral, erotic, ribald, scatological . . . Basically, Funk is concerned with man, and the Funk image of man is the final inversion: man actually turned inside out."[11] The direction is toward perdition. Gentle humor about life's trivial ironies becomes a thrust to the vitals. Even apparently neutral ground is threatened by the "malice of the inanimate object."[12] Nothing is safe, no one is spared.

The artist has created an image of the darkest aspects of man's soul and activities, reacting intuitively to the arrogance, hostility, and complacency which closes in from all sides. He cannot portray the grandeur of humanity when the obvious necessity is to create a deeper sense of the power of evil. Yet, like Henry David Thoreau, he does not "propose to write an ode to dejection." He desperately wants to start a dialogue on humanity's weaknesses, hostilities, ineptitude, with the hope that out of it will come a search for renewal. It is such a rapport that Joseph Raffael seeks: "I heard myself think that it comes down to *The Personal,* exploring and expounding upon the artist's *own* reaction to realistic world, a world outside of him, and what he does is throw out a cable from his inner world: to relate the two, to still for a moment the two, to create an order out of the psychic-visual worlds, to thrust into the outer world the artist's physical manifestation of his spirit solaced, his spirit verified, materialized."[13] Despite society's overwhelming lust for material things, there are still those who espouse faith, hope and charity. Theirs is the realization that by portraying the worst, the survival of human values is still a possibility. With Albert Camus, they know that "we cannot assert the innocence of anyone, whereas we can state with certainty the guilt of all. Every man testifies to the crime of all others— that is my faith and my hope."[14]

Notes to the text

1 In *Violence in Recent American Art,* by Robert Glauber, Museum of Contemporary Art, Chicago, 1968, no pagination.

2 Edward Kienholz: interview with Arthur Secunda, *Artforum,* Vol. 1, No. 5, Oct., 1962, p. 32.

3 In *Letters of Sacco and Vanzetti,* Viking Press, New York, 1928, p. V.

4 Leonard Baskin, "Of Roots and Veins," The Dickinson College Office of Information Services, Carlisle, Pa., 1963, no pagination.

5 In "Beyond Virtuosity," by Henry J. Seldis, in *Rico Lebrun,* Los Angeles County Museum of Art, 1967, p. 27.

6 In *Saul,* by Ellen H. Johnson, Allan Frumkin Gallery, New York, 1964, no pagination.

7 In *Fourteen Americans,* ed., Dorothy Miller, The Museum of Modern Art, New York, 1946, p. 59.

8 Henry T. Tuckerman, *Book of the Artists. American Artist Life,* G. P. Putnam & Son, New York, 1867, p. 429.

9 Lucas Samaras: in "Master of the Object," *Time,* Sept. 20, 1968.

10 Martin Friedman, *Ten American Sculptors,* Walker Art Center, Minneapolis, 1963, no pagination.

11 Harold Paris, "Sweet Land of Funk," *Art In America,* Vol. 55, No. 2, April, 1967, pp. 96, 98.

12 Attributed to F. Th. Vischer in *The Grotesque in Art and Literature,* by Wolfgang Kayser, McGraw-Hill, New York, 1966, p. 110.

13 Joseph Raffael: letter to the author, May 25, 1969.

14 Albert Camus, *The Fall,* Vintage Books, New York, 1956, p. 110.

Edward Kienholz. The Wait.
1964-65. Mixed media. 80 x 148 x 78. Collection of the
Whitney Museum of American Art, New York. Gift of the
Howard and Jean Lipman Foundation, Inc.

Bruce Conner. Child.
1959. Wax, wood, nylon. 35 x 24 x 18. Lent by Philip Johnson

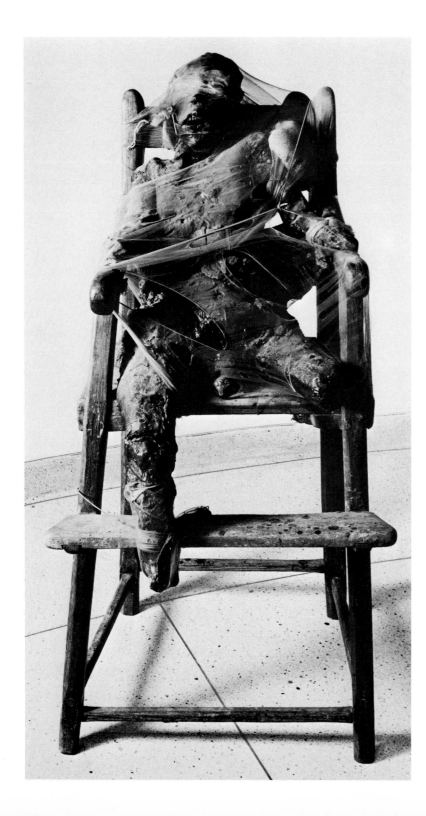

Karl Wirsum. Baseball Girl.
1964. Oil on canvas. 39 x 31. Lent by Mr. and Mrs. Leonard
Horwich

Norman Lundin. A Brief Biography of the Cadez Family—The Father.
1968. Charcoal, acrylic, sanguine on paper. 45½ x 56¼. Lent
by Fountain Gallery, Portland

William Weege. I hope your Mayor isn't a Fascist Pig. 1968. Silkscreen. 80 x 36. Lent by Richard Gray Gallery, Chicago

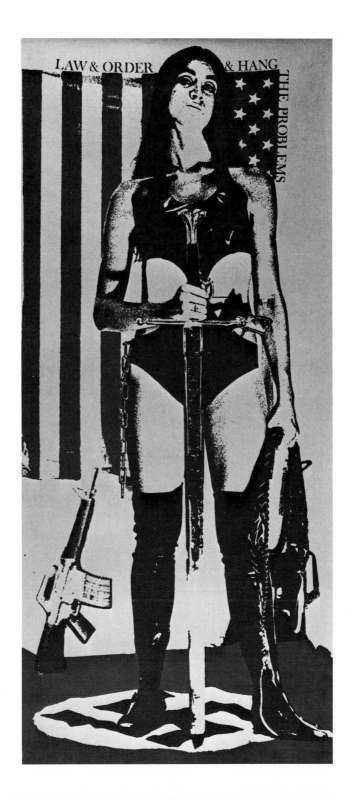

H. C. Westermann. The Evil New War God.
1958. Brass, partly chrome plated. 17 x 15 x 15. Lent by
Howard and Jean Lipman

S. Clay Wilson. The Gypsy Bandits Tangle with the Bike—Freak Dykes.
1967. Ink on paper. 11 x 14. Lent by the artist

Rico Lebrun. Study for Dachau Chamber.
1958. Oil on canvas. 79 x 60. Lent by Lee Nordness Galleries

Lucas Samaras. Untitled Box Number 3.
1963. Mixed media. 24½ x 11½ x 10¼ . Collection of the
Whitney Museum of American Art, New York. Gift of the
Howard and Jean Lipman Foundation, Inc.

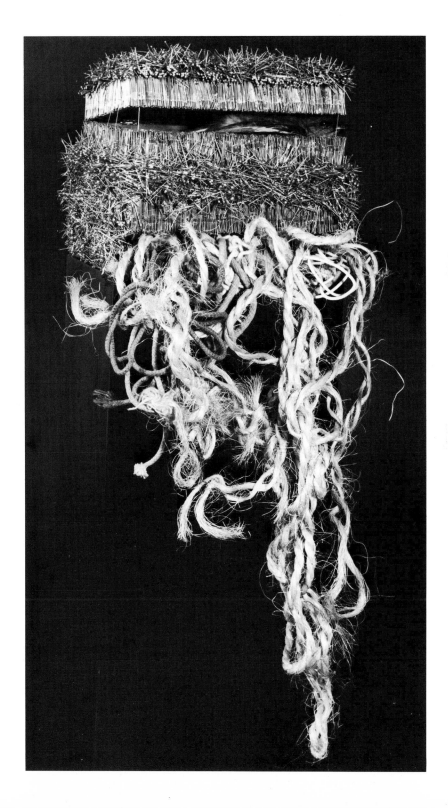

Kerig Pope. Seated Luminary.
1969. Pastel and pencil. 18 x 24. Lent by the artist

Joseph Raffael. Man and Bird.
1969. Oil on canvas and board. 80 x 70. Lent by Stable Gallery

Paul Thek. Death of a Hippie.
1967. Mixed media. 144 x 144 x 102. Lent by Stable Gallery

Paul Thek. Death of a Hippie. (interior.)
1967. Mixed media. 144 x 144 x 102. Lent by Stable Gallery

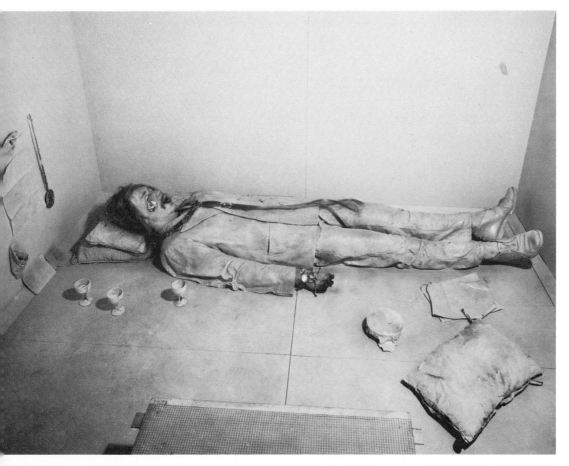

Jerry N. Uelsmann. Untitled.
1968. Photograph. 9¼ x 7¾. Lent by the artist

Ernest Trova. Study Falling Man: 12″ Figure in Shaped Box.
1967. Aluminum, plexiglas. 8½ x 14½ x 21¼ . Lent by Martin
Sosnoff

David Smith. Medals for Dishonor: Bombing Civilian Populations. 1939-40. Bronze. 9 15/16 x 9 15/16. Lent by The Estate of David Smith, courtesy of Marlborough-Gerson Gallery

Peter Saul. Saigon.
1967. Oil on canvas. 93 x 142. Lent by Allan Frumkin Gallery

David Freed. Rumor III.
1968. Etching and stencil. 35 x 17½ . Lent by Associated
American Artists

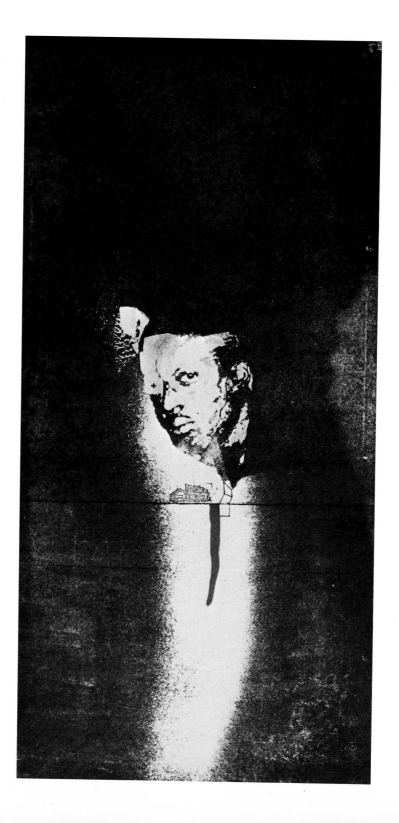

Luis Jiminez. The American Dream.
1968. Fiberglas, epoxy. 58 x 34 x 30. Lent by Graham Gallery

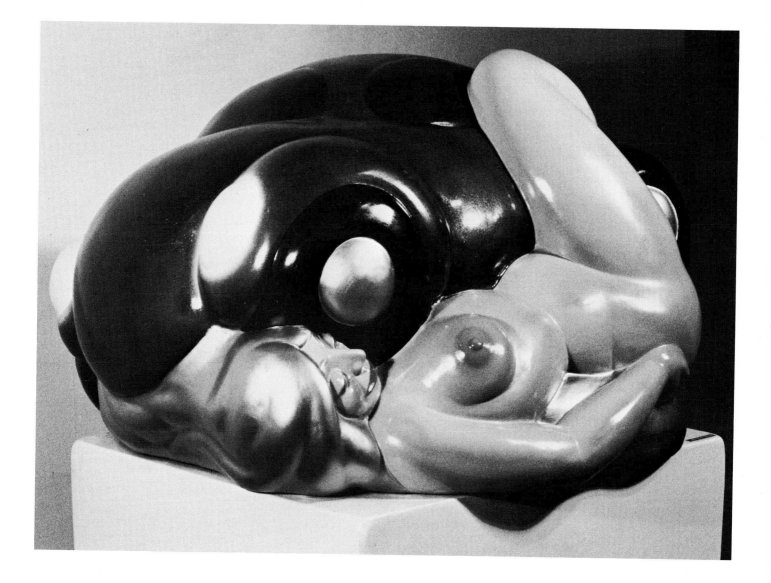

Willem de Kooning. Woman and Bicycle.
1952-53. Oil on canvas. 76½ x 49. Collection of the Whitney
Museum of American Art, New York

Mel Ramos. Hippopotamus.
1967. Oil on canvas. 70 x 96. Lent by David Stuart Galleries

Leonard Baskin. Poet Laureate.
1956. Bronze. 35 x 15 x 5. Lent by Roy R. Neuberger

Gregory Gillespie. Exterior Wall with Landscape.
1967. Oil on canvas. 41 x 25. Lent by Joseph H. Hirshhorn
Foundation

Thomas Nast. Jewels Among Swine.
1874. Wood-engraving. 19½ x 9½. Lent by Mr. and Mrs.
Neil R. Stout

Paul Thek. Untitled.
1967. Mixed media. 9¼ x 35 x 9½ . Lent by Stable Gallery

Edward Kienholz. While Visions of Sugarplums Danced In Their Heads.
1964. Mixed media. 72 x 144 x 108. Lent by Eugenia Butler

Theodore Roszak. Iron Throat.
1959. Steel. 42 x 52 x 22. Lent by Pierre Matisse Gallery

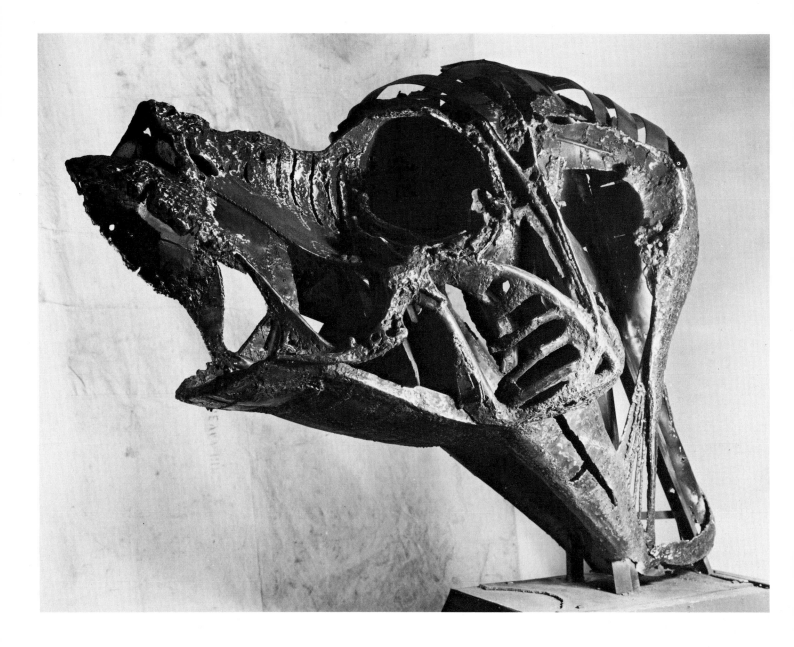

Sidney Goodman. The Walk.
1963. Oil on canvas. 83½ x 65½. Lent by Dr. and Mrs.
Abraham Melamed

Cosmo Campoli. Birth of Death. 1950. Bronze. 33 x 8 x 27.
Lent by Allan Frumkin Gallery

Clayton Pinkerton. American Hero.
1968. Acrylic on plexiglas. 60 x 60. Lent by Arleigh Gallery,
San Francisco

George Tooker. Government Bureau.
1956. Egg tempera on gesso panel. 19⅝ x 29⅝. Lent by The
Metropolitan Museum of Art, George A. Hearn Fund, 1956

William Tunberg. Puddin' Pie, Needle in your Eye.
1969. Mixed media. 72 x 30 x 18. Lent by the artist

Robert Mallary. Sycorax.
1962. Polyester and stone. 99 x 48 x 18. Collection of the
Whitney Museum of American Art, New York. Gift under the
Ford Foundation Purchase Program

Daniel LaRue Johnson. Yesterday.
1963. Mixed media. 26½ x 28¼ x 7½. Lent by the artist

Stephen Greene. The Burial.
1947. Oil on canvas. 42 x 55. Collection of the Whitney
Museum of American Art, New York

David McManaway. The Private Joke.
1968. Mixed media. 25 x 12 x 6. Lent by Murray Smither

Duane Hanson. Riot.
1968. Mixed media. 74 x 240 x 144. Lent by O.K. Harris Gallery

Raoul Middleman. Reclining Nude.
1968. Oil on canvas. 84 x 70½. Lent by Allan Stone Gallery

Robert Crumb. Street Corner Daze.
1968. Ink on paper. Two panels, each 11 x 8½. Lent by the
artist

Jerry Savage. A. R., 1918-1968.
1968. Mixed media. 112 x 151 x 124½. Lent by the artist

Joseph Hirsch. Triptych.
1967-69. Oil on canvas. 16 x 120. Lent by Forum Gallery

Tony Berlant. The Bee in her Bonnet.
1969. Mixed media. 11½ x 10 x 7¼ . Lent by the artist

Tony Berlant. The Bee in her Bonnet (detail).
1969. Mixed media. 11½ x 10 x 7½ . Lent by the artist

Jim Nutt. Miss E. Knows.
1967. Mixed media. 75½ x 51½. Lent by the artist

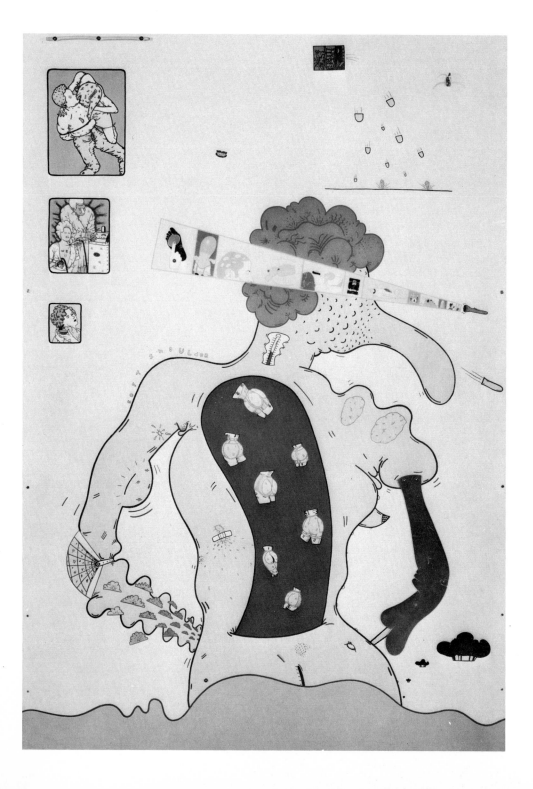

Robert Arneson. Toaster.
1966. Ceramic. 9 x 15 x 10. Lent by Mr. and Mrs. Allan Stone

Harold Persico Paris. Big Mama.
1961. Bronze. 43 x 23 x 21. Lent by Hansen-Fuller Gallery,
San Francisco

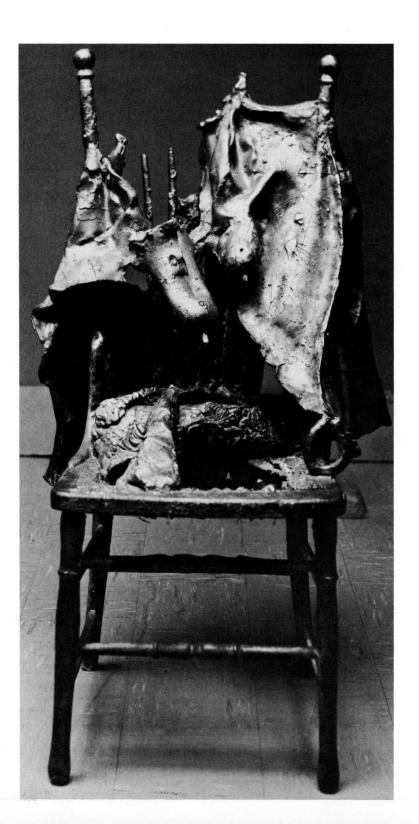

Gladys Nilsson. Catwomen War.
1968. Watercolor. 31 x 22½. Lent by the artist

Nancy Grossman. Male Figure.
1969. Ink on paper. 35 x 23. Lent by Cordier & Ekstrom, Inc.

Ivan Le Lorraine Albright. The Temptation of Saint Anthony.
1944-45. Oil on canvas. 50 x 60. Lent by Kennedy
Galleries, Inc.

Catalogue

Measurements are in inches, height preceding width and depth. The Asterisk indicates that the work will also be shown at the University Art Museum, University of California, Berkeley. Number 68 will be shown in Berkeley only. Galleries and the artist's residence are located in New York unless indicated otherwise.

Abeles, Sigmund. b. 1934. Wellesley, Mass.
1 Gift of America Series II: Napalm. 1967.* Etching. 23½ x 15½. Lent by Associated American Artists

Albright, Ivan Le Lorraine. b. 1897. Chicago, Ill.
2 The Temptation of Saint Anthony. 1944-45. Oil on canvas. 50 x 60. Lent by Kennedy Galleries, Inc.

Antonakos, Stephen. b. 1926.
3 Dream Pillow. 1963. Mixed media. 15 x 22 x 8. Lent by Miss Eva Hesse

Arbus, Diane. b. 1923.
4 Birdmask. 1969.* Photograph. 20 x 16. Lent by the artist
5 Christmas Tree, Levittown. 1962.* Photograph. 20 x 16. Lent by the artist
6 Transvestite at Home. 1966.* Photograph. 20 x 16. Lent by the artist

Arneson, Robert. b. 1930. Davis, Cal.
7 Call Girl. 1965.* Painted ceramic. 24 x 8 x 8. Lent by Hansen-Fuller Gallery, San Francisco
8 Toaster. 1966.* Ceramic. 9 x 15 x 10. Lent by Mr. and Mrs. Allan Stone

Bardazzi, Peter. b. 1943.
9 Goyt. 1969.* Acrylic on canvas. 96 x 72. Lent by the artist

Baskin, Leonard. b. 1922. Northampton, Mass.
10 Glutted Death. 1959.* Bronze. 16½ x 8 x 2. Lent by Howard and Jean Lipman
11 Poet Laureate. 1956.* Bronze. 9½ x 12 x 5. Lent by Roy R. Neuberger
12 Seated Birdman. 1961.* Bronze. 35 x 15 x 20. Lent by Howard and Jean Lipman
13 Tormented Man. 1956.* Ink and watercolor. 39½ x 26½. Collection of the Whitney Museum of American Art, New York. Living Arts Foundation Fund

Bellows, George. 1882-1925.
14 The Drunk. 1924.* Lithograph. 15½ x 13. Lent by Associated American Artists

Berlant, Tony. b. 1941. Santa Monica, Cal.
15 Gluttony. 1969.* Mixed media. 11½ x 10 x 7½. Lent by the artist
16 Death in Los Angeles. 1968.* Mixed media. 15 x 10 x 14. Lent by the artist
17 Love Slave. 1969.* Mixed media. 11½ x 10 x 7½. Lent by the artist
18 The Bee in her Bonnet. 1969.* Mixed media. 11½ x 10 x 7½. Lent by the artist

Berman, Eugene. b. 1899. Rome, Italy.
19 Muse of the Western World. 1942.* Oil on canvas. 50⅞ x 37¾. Lent by The Metropolitan Museum of Art. George A. Hearn Fund, 1943

Blackwell, Thomas. b. 1938.
20 Gook. 1969. Oil on canvas with assemblage. 79 x 97. Lent by the artist

Bloom, Hyman. b. 1913. Boston, Mass.
21 The Anatomist. 1953. Oil on canvas. 70½ x 40½. Collection of the Whitney Museum of American Art, New York

Cadmus, Paul. b. 1904. Brooklyn, N. Y.
22 Bar Italia. 1955.* Tempera, 37½ x 45½. Lent by National Collection of Fine Arts, S. C. Johnson Collection
23 Coney Island. 1935.* Oil on canvas. 32¾ x 36¼. Lent by Peter A. Paanakker and the Los Angeles County Museum of Art

Castellon, Federico. b. 1914.
24 The Dark Figure. 1938.* Oil on canvas. 17 x 26⅛. Collection of the Whitney Museum of American Art, New York

Campoli, Cosmo. b. 1922. Chicago, Ill.
25 Birth of Death. 1950.* Bronze. 33 x 8 x 27. Lent by Allan Frumkin Gallery

Conner, Bruce. b. 1933. San Francisco, Cal.
26 Child. 1959. Wax, wood, nylon. 35 x 24 x 18. Lent by Philip Johnson
27 Medusa. 1960. Mixed media. 10¾ x 11 x 22¼. Collection of the Whitney Museum of American Art, New York. Gift of Howard and Jean Lipman Foundation, Inc.
28 Wednesday. 1960.* Mixed media. 83 x 19 x 23½. Lent by Peter Selz

Craig, John. b. 1943. Chicago, Ill.
29 Hide Me In Your Cloak, Daddy. 1967. Wood-engraving. 4½ x 3¾. Lent by Phyllis Kind Gallery, Chicago
30 Untitled. 1967. Wood-engraving. 4 x 4. Lent by Phyllis Kind Gallery, Chicago

Crumb, Robert. b. 1943. San Francisco, Cal.
31 Stoned. 1968. Ink on paper. Four panels, each 10 x 7. Lent by Michael Stepanian

32 Street Corner Daze. 1968. Ink on paper. Two panels, each 11 x 8½. Lent by the artist

33 Whiteman. 1968. Ink on paper. Four panels, each 11 x 8½. Lent by Michael Stepanian

de Kooning, Willem. b. 1904. Easthampton, N. Y.

34 Untitled. 1969.* Charcoal on paper. 18¾ x 24. Lent by M. Knoedler & Co., Inc.

35 Untitled. 1969.* Charcoal on paper. 18¾ x 24. Lent by M. Knoedler & Co., Inc.

36 Untitled. 1969.* Charcoal on paper. 24 x 18¾. Lent by M. Knoedler & Co., Inc.

37 Woman and Bicycle. 1952-53.* Oil on canvas. 76½ x 49. Collection of the Whitney Museum of American Art, New York

Ferrara, Jackie. b. 1929.

38 Bobcat Skull. 1969. Mixed media. 44 x 10 x 4. Lent by the artist

39 Untitled. 1968.* Mixed media. 84 x 16 x 7. Lent by Mr. and Mrs. Allan Stone

Freed, David. b. 1936. Richmond, Va.

40 Rumor III. 1968.* Etching and stencil. 35 x 17½. Lent by Associated American Artists

Gillespie, Gregory. b. 1936. Rome, Italy.

41 Double Portrait. 1967.* Mixed media. 10 x 6¾. Lent by Forum Gallery

42 Exterior Wall with Landscape. 1967. Oil on canvas. 41 x 25. Lent by Joseph H. Hirshhorn Foundation

Goodman, Sidney. b. 1936. Philadelphia, Pa.

43 Sanctuary. 1961. Watercolor. 24½ x 33¾. Lent by Philadelphia Museum of Art

44 Shelter. 1961. Watercolor. 29½ x 22. Lent by Mr. and Mrs. William Marsteller

45 The Walk. 1963.* Oil on canvas. 83½ x 65½. Lent by Dr. and Mrs. Abraham Melamed

46 Zone. 1969.* Charcoal on paper. 25 x 32. Lent by Terry Dintenfass, Inc.

Grashow, James. b. 1942.

47 Godiva. 1967. Wood-engraving. 13 x 15. Lent by Allan Stone Gallery

48 No More War. 1968.* Wood-engraving. 47 x 38. Lent by Allan Stone Gallery

Green, Art. b. 1941. Chicago, Ill.

49 Absolute Purity. 1967. Oil on canvas. 120 x 60. Lent by the artist

Greenbaum, Marty. b. 1934.

50 16 Guns. 1968. Mixed media. 22½ x 24 x 4. Lent by Paula Cooper Gallery

Greene, Stephen. b. 1918. Valley Cottage, N. Y.

51 The Burial. 1947.* Oil on canvas. 42 x 55. Collection of the Whitney Museum of American Art, New York

Grossman, Nancy. b. 1940.

52 Male Figure. 1969. Ink on paper. 35 x 23. Lent by Cordier & Ekstrom, Inc.

53 T. U. F. 1969.* Leather, steel, wood. 21 x 7½ x 11. Lent by Mrs. McFadden Staempfli

Grosz, George. 1893-1959.

54 After the Questioning. 1935. Watercolor. 17¼ x 22¾. Lent by Mr. Arnott J. White

55 Waving the Flag. 1947-48.* Watercolor. 25 x 18. Collection of the Whitney Museum of American Art, New York

Hanson, Duane. b. 1925.

56 Pieta. 1969.* Mixed media. 59 x 56 x 38. Lent by O. K. Harris Gallery

57 Riot. 1968. Mixed media. 74 x 240 x 144. Lent by O. K. Harris Gallery

Hedrick, Wally. b. 1928. San Francisco, Cal.

58 Madame Nhu's Bar-B-Q's. 1962.* Oil on canvas. 67 x 48. Lent by the artist

Henderson, William Howard, Jr. b. 1943, San Francisco, Cal.

59 Non-Violent. 1968.* Oil on canvas. 72 x 120. Lent by the artist

Hirsch, Joseph. b. 1910.

60 Triptych. 1967-69.* Oil on canvas. 16 x 120. Lent by Forum Gallery

Israel, Marvin. b. 1924.

61 Untitled. 1968. Acrylic and pastel on cardboard. 51 x 40. Collection of the Whitney Museum of American Art, New York. Anonymous Purchase Fund

62 Untitled. 1969.* Acrylic on paper. 42 x 30. Lent by Cordier & Ekstrom, Inc.

Jiminez, Luis. b. 1940.

63 Oedipal Dream. 1968.* Colored pencil on paper. 22 x 16. Lent by Alfonso Ossorio

64 Tank. 1968.* Fiberglas, epoxy. 48 x 36 x 30. Lent by Graham Gallery

65 The American Dream. 1968.* Fiberglas, epoxy. 58 x 34 x 30. Lent by Graham Gallery

Johnson, Daniel LaRue. b. 1938.

66 Giving It Back. 1964.* Mixed media. 32 x 15 x 4½. Lent by Mrs. Diana Zlotnick

67 Yesterday. 1963.* Mixed media. 26½ x 28¼ x 7½. Lent by the artist

Kienholz, Edward. b. 1927. Los Angeles, Cal.

68 Eleventh Hour Final. 1968.* Mixed media. 96 x 168 x 192. Collection of the University Art Museum, University of California, Berkeley

69 The Wait. 1964-65. Mixed media. 80 x 148 x 78. Collection of the Whitney Museum of American Art, New York. Gift of the Howard and Jean Lipman Foundation, Inc.

70 While Visions of Sugarplums Danced In Their Heads. 1964. Mixed media. 72 x 144 x 108. Lent by Eugenia Butler, Los Angeles

Koerner, Henry. b. 1915. Pittsburgh, Pa.

71 Vanity Fair. 1946. Oil on composition board. 36 x 42. Collection of the Whitney Museum of American Art, New York

Kriesberg, Irving. b. 1919.

72 Escalation. 1967. Oil on canvas. 50 x 216. Lent by the artist

Kupchinskas, Richard. b. 1943.

73 Untitled. 1968. Mixed media. 40 x 36 x 36. Lent by the artist

Landau, Jacob. b. 1917. Roosevelt, N. J.

74 Holocaust Suite: The Question. 1968.* Lithograph. 15 x 19¼. Lent by Associated American Artists

Leaf, June. b. 1929.

75 Eve and Desire. 1968. Mixed media on paper. 22½ x 28½. Lent by Allan Frumkin Gallery

76 LBJ as a Cornerstone for a New Theatre. 1967. Mixed media on paper. 28½ x 22½. Lent by Allan Frumkin Gallery

77 Woman Theatre. 1968.* Mixed media. 84 x 56 x 5. Lent by Allan Frumkin Gallery

Lebrun, Rico. 1900-64.

78 Bound Figure. 1962.* Bronze. 7½ x 11 x 8. Lent by Lee Nordness Galleries

79 Study for Dachau Chamber. 1958.* Oil on canvas. 79 x 85. Lent by Lee Nordness Galleries

Lindner, Richard. b. 1901.

80 Double Portrait. 1965.* Oil on canvas. 40 x 60. Lent by Miss Helen Mary Harding

81 Leopard Lily. 1966. Watercolor. 40 x 28¼. Lent by Miss Helen Mary Harding

Lundin, Norman. b. 1940. Seattle, Wash.

82 A Brief Biography of the Cadez Family—The Father. 1968.* Charcoal, acrylic, sanguine on paper. 45½ x 56¼. Lent by Fountain Gallery, Portland

83 Study—A Brief Biography of the Cadez Family—The Son. 1968.* Charcoal, acrylic on paper. 36 x 45¼. Lent by Seligman Gallery, Seattle

Mallary, Robert. b. 1917. New Rochelle, N. Y.

84 Marsyas. 1963.* Mixed media. 78 x 72 x 60. Lent by Allan Stone Gallery

85 Sycorax. 1962. Polyester, stone. 99 x 48 x 18. Collection of the Whitney Museum of American Art, New York. Gift under the Ford Foundation Purchase Program

Maryan. b. 1927.

86 Donkey Personage. 1962.* Oil on canvas. 50 x 50. Lent by Allan Frumkin Gallery

87 Personage with Candy Cane. 1969. Oil on canvas. 60 x 60. Lent by Allan Frumkin Gallery

Mazur, Michael. b. 1935. Cambridge, Mass.

88 Images From a Locked Ward: The Room For Sleeping. 1963-65.* Lithograph. 18 x 23¾. Lent by Associated American Artists

McKeevy, Byron. b. 1936. Covington, Ky.

89 Birdseye. 1968. Lithograph. 26 x 19. Lent by Phyllis Kind Gallery, Chicago

90 General Gourmet. 1968. Lithograph. 30 x 22. Lent by Phyllis Kind Gallery, Chicago

McManaway, David. b. 1927. Dallas, Texas

91 Jomo Box. 1969. Mixed media. 11 x 60 x 6. Lent by Atelier Chapman Kelley, Dallas

92 The Private Joke. 1968.* Mixed media. 25 x 12 x 6. Lent by Murray Smither

Middleman, Raoul. b. 1935.

93 Reclining Nude. 1968.* Oil on canvas. 84 x 70½. Lent by Allan Stone Gallery

Nast, Thomas. 1840-1902.

94 In Memoriam—Our Civil Service as It Was. 1877.* Wood-engraving. 19½ x 9½. Lent by Mr. and Mrs. Neil R. Stout

95 Jewels Among Swine. 1874.* Wood-engraving. 19½ x 9½. Lent by Mr. and Mrs. Neil R. Stout

96 "Let Us Clasp Hands Over the Bloody Chasm". 1872.* Wood-engraving. 9½ x 14½. Lent by Mr. and Mrs. Neil R. Stout

97 "The Day We Celebrate"—(April 1). 1877.* Wood-engraving. 10¾ x 9. Lent by Mr. and Mrs. Neil R. Stout
98 The Web of Ruin. 1877.* Wood-engraving. 14½ x 9½. Lent by Mr. and Mrs. Neil R. Stout

Nilsson, Gladys. b. 1940. Sacramento, Cal.
99 Blewbanananosmask. 1968.* Watercolor. 22½ x 31. Lent by the artist
100 Catwomen War. 1968.* Watercolor. 31 x 22½. Lent by the artist
101 Decalkomanea Ptng. in 3 Colors. 1969.* Watercolor. 22½ x 31. Lent by the artist
102 Subterrachial Bop Boop. 1967.* Watercolor. 31 x 22½. Lent by the artist
103 Sweepee Ptng. 1969.* Watercolor. 31 x 22½. Lent by the artist

Nowack, Wayne. b. 1926. North Hollywood, Cal.
104 Mysterium Coniunctionis. 1967. Mixed media. 14 x 11 x 11. Lent by Mr. and Mrs. Allan Stone

Nutt, Jim. b. 1938. Sacramento, Cal.
105 Da Vicious Roomer. 1968.* Acrylic on plexiglas and enamel on wood. 36 x 34. Lent by the artist
106 Miss E. Knows. 1967.* Mixed media. 75½ x 51½. Lent by the artist
107 She's Hit. 1967.* Acrylic on plexiglas and enamel on wood. 26½ x 24½. Lent by the artist
108 Why did He doo it? 1967.* Acrylic on plexiglas and enamel on wood. 61 x 37. Lent by the artist

Ossorio, Alfonso. b. 1916. Easthampton, N. Y.
109 Birth. 1949.* Wax and watercolor on paper. 40 x 30. Lent by Miss Helen Mary Harding
110 Inxit, 2/Yang & Yin 69. 1969.* Mixed media. 168 x 150 x 24. Lent by Cordier & Ekstrom, Inc.
111 Purple Skull. 1941. Watercolor on paper. 16 x 10½. Lent by the artist

Ortiz, Ralph. b. 1934.
112 Archaeological Find, Number 9. 1964. Mixed media. 77 x 64 x 23. Collection of the Whitney Museum of American Art, New York. Gift of George and Lillian Schwartz

Paris, Harold Persico. b. 1925. Berkeley, Cal.
113 Beggar. 1961.* Bronze. 14 x 36 x 22. Lent by Hansen-Fuller Gallery, San Francisco
114 Big Mama. 1961.* Bronze. 43 x 23 x 21. Lent by Hansen-Fuller Gallery, San Francisco

Paschke, Ed. b. 1939. Chicago, Ill.
115 Dos Criados. 1968.* Oil on canvas. 48 x 40. Lent by the artist
116 Fat Lady. 1968.* Oil on canvas. 40 x 50. Lent by Mr. and Mrs. Edwin Bergman
117 Tet Inoffensive. 1968.* Oil on canvas. 38 x 34. Lent by the artist

Pinkerton, Clayton. b. 1931. Richmond, Cal.
118 American Hero. 1968.* Acrylic on plexiglas. 60 x 60. Lent by Arleigh Gallery, San Francisco
119 Cell. 1968.* Acrylic on masonite. 96 x 48. Lent by Arleigh Gallery, San Francisco

Pope, Kerig. b. 1935. Chicago, Ill.
120 Fiends Resting. 1967.* Pencil. 18 x 24. Lent by the artist
121 Seated Luminary. 1969.* Pastel, pencil. 18 x 24. Lent by the artist
122 Secluded Snailery. 1969.* Pastel, pencil. 18 x 24. Lent by the artist
123 Singing Furniture. 1968.* Pastel. 18 x 24. Lent by the artist

Raffael, Joseph. b. 1933. Bennington, Vt.
124 Baggie, Covered Baby, Face, Covered Face. 1967.* Mixed media. 58¾ x 60. Lent by Stable Gallery
125 Man and Bird. 1969.* Oil on canvas and board. 80 x 70. Lent by Stable Gallery

Ramos, Mel. b. 1935. Oakland, Cal.
126 Hippopotamus. 1967.* Oil on canvas. 70 x 96. Lent by David Stuart Galleries, Los Angeles, Cal.

Rollins, Henry. b. 1937. San Francisco, Cal.
127 The New Eye. 1967-69.* Mixed media. 36 x 18 x 18. Lent by the artist

Rosofsky, Seymour. b. 1924. Chicago, Ill.
128 The Beach Card Party. 1968.* Lithograph. 29 x 42. Lent by Phyllis Kind Gallery, Chicago
129 The General. 1968.* Lithograph. 32 x 24¼. Lent by Phyllis Kind Gallery, Chicago
130 The Good Burghers of Lunidam (Number 2). 1968.* Lithograph. 24 x 32. Lent by Phyllis Kind Gallery, Chicago
131 The Good Burghers of Lunidam (Number 7). 1968.* Lithograph. 24 x 32. Lent by Phyllis Kind Gallery, Chicago

Roszak, Theodore. b. 1907.
132 Iron Throat. 1959.* Steel. 42 x 52 x 22. Lent by Pierre Matisse Gallery

Samaras, Lucas. b. 1936.

133 Box Number 38. 1966. Mixed media. 8 x 12 x 9. Lent by Private Collection

134 Untitled Box Number 3. 1963.* Mixed media. 24½ x 11½ x 10¼. Collection of the Whitney Museum of American Art, New York. Gift of the Howard and Jean Lipman Foundation, Inc.

135 Untitled Sculpture. 1962. Mixed media. 5½ x 11⅜ x 8⅞. Lent by Philip Johnson

Saul, Peter. b. 1934. Mill Valley, Cal.

136 Saigon. 1967.* Oil on canvas. 93 x 142. Lent by Allan Frumkin Gallery

Savage, Jerry. b. 1936. Urbana, Ill.

137 A. R., 1918-1968. 1968.* Mixed media. 112 x 151 x 124½. Lent by the artist

Smith, David. 1906-1965.

138 Medals for Dishonor: Bombing Civilian Populations. 1939.* Bronze. 9 15/16 x 9 15/16. Lent by The Estate of David Smith, courtesy of Marlborough-Gerson Gallery

139 Medals for Dishonor: Cooperation of the Clergy. 1939.* Bronze. 10½ x 10¼. Lent by The Estate of David Smith, courtesy of Marlborough-Gerson Gallery

140 Medals for Dishonor: Death by Bacteria. 1939.* Bronze. 8¾ x 10½. Lent by The Estate of David Smith, courtesy of Marlborough-Gerson Gallery

141 Medals for Dishonor: Death by Gas. 1939-40. Bronze. 10¼ x 11¼. Lent by Joseph H. Hirshhorn Collection

142 Medals for Dishonor: Diplomats. 1938-39.* Silver. 9¾ x 9¾. Lent by The Estate of David Smith, courtesy of Marlborough-Gerson Gallery

143 Medals for Dishonor: Elements which Cause Prostitution. 1939.* Bronze. 8¾ x 10½. Lent by The Estate of David Smith, courtesy of Marlborough-Gerson Gallery

144 Medals for Dishonor: Food Trust. 1938.* Bronze. 7¼ x 14. Lent by The Estate of David Smith, courtesy of Marlborough-Gerson Gallery

145 Medals for Dishonor: Munition Makers. 1939.* Bronze. 9¾ x 9¾. Lent by The Estate of David Smith, courtesy of Marlborough-Gerson Gallery

146 Medals for Dishonor: Propaganda for War. 1939-40.* Bronze. 9½ x 11½. Lent by The Estate of David Smith, courtesy of Marlborough-Gerson Gallery

147 Medals for Dishonor: Reaction in Medicine. 1940.* Bronze. 8¾ x 10⅛. Lent by The Estate of David Smith, courtesy of Marlborough-Gerson Gallery

148 Medals for Dishonor: Scientific Body Disposal. 1939-40.* Bronze. 10 x 10. Lent by The Estate of David Smith, courtesy of Marlborough-Gerson Gallery

149 Medals for Dishonor: Sinking Hospital and Civilian Refugee Ships. 1939.* Bronze. 8½ x 12¼. Lent by The Estate of David Smith, courtesy of Marlborough-Gerson Gallery

150 Medals for Dishonor: The Fourth Estate: 1939-40.* Bronze. 8⅝ x 10½. Lent by The Estate of David Smith, courtesy of Marlborough-Gerson Gallery

151 Medals for Dishonor: War Exempt Sons of the Rich. 1939-40.* Bronze. 10¼ x 9⅛. Lent by The Estate of David Smith, courtesy of Marlborough-Gerson Gallery

152 Medals for Dishonor: Private Law and Order Leagues. 1939.* Bronze. 10½ x 10½. Lent by The Estate of David Smith, courtesy of Marlborough-Gerson Gallery

Sommer, Frederick. b. 1905. Prescott, Ariz.

153 Artificial Leg. 1944.* Photograph. 9½ x 7½. Lent by The Museum of Modern Art, New York

154 Coyotes. 1941.* Photograph. 7⅝ x 9⅝. Lent by The Museum of Modern Art, New York. Gift of the artist

155 Still Life. 1938.* Photograph. 9½ x 7⅝. Lent by The Museum of Modern Art, New York. Nelson A. Rockefeller Fund

Spain. b. 1940.

156 Manning. 1969.* Ink on paper. Four panels, each 21½ x 15½. Lent by the artist

Steckel, Anita. b. 1930.

157 Monster Head Number 1. 1961. Watercolor, pencil on paper. 21½ x 18. Lent by the artist

158 Monster Head Number 2. 1961. Watercolor, pencil on paper. 12 x 12. Lent by the artist

Stiegelmeyer, Norman. b. 1937. Mill Valley, Cal.
159 Transformation of William Burroughs. 1966.* Acrylic on canvas.
46 x 36. Lent by the artist

Thek, Paul. b. 1933.
160 Death of a Hippie. 1967. Mixed media. 144 x 144 x 102. Lent by
Stable Gallery
161 Untitled. 1967.* Mixed media. 26 x 14½ x 8. Lent by Stable Gallery
162 Untitled. 1967.* Mixed media. 9¼ x 35 x 9½. Lent by Stable Gallery

Tooker, George. b. 1920. Hartland, Vt.
163 Government Bureau. 1956.* Egg tempera on gesso panel. 19⅝ x 29⅝.
Lent by The Metropolitan Museum of Art, George A. Hearn Fund, 1956

Trova, Ernest. b. 1927. St. Louis, Mo.
164 Falling Man Study: Mirrored Landscape #87. 1968. Brass, glass.
16½ x 34½ x 17. Lent by Private Collection
165 Study: Falling Man on Time Machine. 1966. Mixed metal. 14 x 14 x 16.
Lent by Miss Karen Sperling
166 Study Falling Man: 12″ Figure in Shaped Box. 1967. Aluminum,
plexiglas. 8½ x 14½ x 21¼. Lent by Martin Sosnoff

Truss, Ned. b. 1939.
167 Untitled. 1968. Watercolor, ink on paper. 12 x 11½. Lent by
the artist

Tunberg, William. b. 1936. Santa Monica, Cal.
168 Puddin' Pie, Needle in your Eye. 1969.* Mixed media. 72 x 30 x 18.
Lent by the artist
169 The National Skeleton in the Closet Syndrome. 1969.* Mixed media.
77 x 60 x 20. Lent by the artist

Uelsmann, Jerry N. b. 1934. Gainsville, Fla.
170 Bless Our Home and Eagle. 1962.* Photograph. 13¼ x 10¼.
Lent by the artist
171 Untitled. 1968.* Photograph. 9¼ x 7¾. Lent by the artist
172 Untitled. 1968.* Photograph. 13½ x 10. Lent by the artist

von Heune, Stephan. b. 1932. Los Angeles, Cal.
173 Coming Through the Rye Bread. 1964. Mixed media. 5½ x 17 x 14.
Lent by the Stanley Grinstein Family

Waterstreet, Ken. b. 1940. Sacramento, Cal.
174 Lipstick Ad Number 50. 1968.* Oil on canvas. 48 x 72½. Lent by
the artist.

Weege, William. b. 1935. Black Earth, Wis.
175 I hope your Mayor isn't a Fascist Pig. 1968.* Silkscreen. 80 x 36.
Lent by Richard Gray Gallery, Chicago
176 Long Live Life—1984. 1968. Silkscreen and photo-offset. 86½ x 107.
Lent by Richard Gray Gallery, Chicago

Westermann, H. C. b. 1922. Brookfield Center, Conn.
177 The Evil New War God. 1958. Brass, partly chrome plated. 17 x 15 x 15.
Lent by Howard and Jean Lipman

Wilson, May. b. 1905.
178 Webbed. 1968. Mixed media. 18 x 10 x 9. Lent by the artist
179 Western. 1967. Mixed media. 18 x 12 x 17. Lent by the artist

Wilson, S. Clay. b. 1941. San Francisco, Cal.
180 Demon with Dental Pick. 1968.* Ink on paper. 12 x 18. Lent by
the artist
181 Demons on Motorcycles. 1967.* Ink on paper. 11 x 14. Lent by
the artist
182 The Gypsy Bandits Tangle with the Bike—Freak Dykes. 1967.*
Ink on paper. 11 x 14. Lent by the artist
183 They Hope to Die Before Getting Old. 1967.* Ink on paper. 11 x 14.
Lent by the artist

Wirsum, Karl. b. 1939. Chicago, Ill.
184 Baseball Girl. 1964.* Oil on canvas. 39 x 31. Lent by Mr. and Mrs.
Leonard Horwich
185 Mane and Hairdress. 1969.* Acrylic on canvas. 48 x 36. Lent by
the artist
186 Show Girl I. 1969.* Acrylic on canvas. 37 x 24. Lent by the artist
187 Show Girl II. 1969.* Acrylic on canvas. 38 x 24. Lent by the artist

Selected Bibliography

References are arranged alphabetically by author, if known, or by title, with exhibition catalogues listed either under the name of the artist exhibited, or (in the case of group shows) the institution which prepared the catalogue or the city in which the institution is located. The place of publication is New York City unless otherwise stated. Libby W. Seaberg compiled the bibliography.

Books and Exhibition Catalogues

Albright, Ivan. *Ivan Albright* (text by Frederick A. Sweet; commentary by Jean Dubuffet translated by Josephine Patterson Albright; foreword by John Maxon; and a statement by the artist). Chicago, Art Institute, 1964.

Baskin, Leonard. *Leonard Baskin* (introduction by Rico Lebrun; essay by Julius Held). Brunswick, Maine, Bowdoin College, 1962.

Bellows, George W. *George W. Bellows; His Lithographs* (essays by Thomas Beer, Eugene Speicher and Atherton Curtis). Alfred A. Knopf, Inc., 1927.

Cadmus, Paul. *Paul Cadmus/Prints and Drawings 1922-1967* (text by Una E. Johnson; research by Jo Miller). Brooklyn, New York, The Brooklyn Museum, 1968.

California, University at Berkeley, University Art Museum. *Funk* (text by Peter Selz). 1967.

Chicago, Museum of Contemporary Art. *Violence in Recent American Art* (introduction by Jan van der Marck; essay by Robert Glauber). 1968.

Conner, Bruce. *Bruce Conner* (introduction by Thomas H. Garver). Waltham, Massachusetts, Brandeis University, The Poses Institute of Fine Arts, 1965.

Dubuffet, Jean. *Peintures Initiatiques d'Alfonso Ossorio.* Paris, La Pierre Volante, 1951.

Finch College, Museum of Art. *Destruction Art* (introduction by Elayne H. Varian), 1968.

Grosz, George. *George Grosz* (text by John I. H. Baur; research by Rosalind Irvine). The Macmillan Company for the Whitney Museum of American Art, 1954.

Grosz, George. *A Little Yes and a Big No;* an autobiography illustrated by the author (Lola Sachs Dorin, trans.). The Dial Press, 1946.

Hirsch, Joseph. *Joseph Hirsch* (statement by the artist). Forum Gallery, 1969.

Kayser, Wolfgang. *The Grotesque in Art* (Ulrich Weisstein, trans.). McGraw-Hill Book Company, 1966.

Keller, Morton. *The Art and Politics of Thomas Nast.* Oxford University Press, 1968.

Kienholz, Edward. *Edward Kienholz* (essay by Maurice Tuchman). Los Angeles, Los Angeles County Museum of Art, 1966.

Kienholz, Edward. *Works from the 1960's by Edward Kienholz* (foreword by Walter Hopps; statement by Marcus G. Raskin). Washington, D.C., Washington Gallery of Modern Art, 1967.

Lebrun, Rico. *Rico Lebrun (1900-1964)* (essays by Henry J. Seldis and Peter Selz). Los Angeles, Los Angeles County Museum of Art, 1967.

Lindner, Richard. *Richard Lindner* (foreword by Rolf Wedewer; essays by Wieland Schmied, Rolf-Gunter Dienst, Sidney Tillim and Roland Penrose; and statements by the artist). Leverkusen, Germany, Städtisches Museum Leverkusen, Schloss Morsbroich, 1968.

Mallary, Robert. *Mallary* (foreword by Benedict Goldsmith; text by Mark Roskill). New York, State University at Potsdam, n.d.

New York, The Museum of Modern Art. *New Images of Man* (text by Peter Selz). 1959.

Samaras, Lucas. *Lucas Samaras* (text by Lawrence Alloway). The Pace Gallery, 1966.

Saul, Peter. *Saul* (essay by Ellen H. Johnson). Allan Frumkin Gallery, 1964.

Smith, David. *Medals for Dishonor* (foreword by William Blake and Christina Stead). Willard Gallery, 1940.

Sommer, Frederick. *Frederick Sommer* (introduction by George D. Culler; essay by Gerald Nordland). Philadelphia, Philadelphia College of Art, 1968.

Trova, Ernest. *Ernest Trova* (foreword by Morton D. May). St. Louis, Famous-Barr Company, 1964.

Trova, Ernest. *Trova* (text by Lawrence Alloway). The Pace Gallery, 1966.

Walker Art Center, Minneapolis. *Eight Sculptors* (introduction and essays on Lucas Samaras and H. C. Westermann by Martin Friedman; essay on Ernest Trova by Jan van der Marck). 1966.

Westermann, Horace Clifford. *H. C. Westermann* (statement by Dennis Adrian). Chicago, Allan Frumkin Gallery, n.d.

Westermann, Horace Clifford. *H. C. Westermann* (foreword by Maurice Tuchman; text by Max Kozloff). Los Angeles, Los Angeles County Museum of Art, 1968.

Periodicals

Ashton, Dore. "Response to Crisis in American Art," *Art in America,* Vol. 57, January-February 1969, pp. 24-33.

Ashton, Dore. "Richard Lindner's Eternal Return," *Arts Magazine,* Vol. 43, May 1969, pp. 48-50.

Dulac, Margarita Walker. "Ivan Albright: Mystic-Realist," *American Artist,* Vol. 30, January 1966, pp. 32-37, 73-74 and 76.

Friedman, B. H. "Alfonso Ossorio," *Art International,* Vol. 6, April 1962, pp. 28-36.

Kind, Joshua. "Albright: Humanist of decay," *Art News,* Vol. 63, November 1964, pp. 43-45, 68-70.

Kuh, Katharine. " 'No Single Fact Is As It Seems,' " *Saturday Review,* Vol. 50, February 11, 1967, pp. 23-27.

Paris, Harold. "Sweet Land of Funk," *Art in America,* Vol. 55, March-April 1967, pp. 94-96.

Plunkett, Edward. "Seymour Rosofsky," *Art Scene,* Vol. 2, February 1969, pp. 6-11.

Saul, Peter and Joe Raffaele. "Los Angeles: Subversive Art," *Arts Magazine,* Vol. 41, May 1967, pp. 50-52.

Solomon, Alan. "An Interview with Lucas Samaras," *Artforum,* Vol. 5, October 1966, pp. 39-44.

Swenson, G. R. "Beneath the Skin," *Art News,* Vol. 65, April 1966, pp. 34-35, 66-67.

Tuchman, Maurice. "A Decade of Edward Kienholz," *Artforum,* Vol. 4, April 1966, pp. 41-45.

Waldman, Diane. "Samaras: Reliquaries for St. Sade," *Art News,* Vol. 65, October 1966, pp. 44-46, 72-75.

Wight, Frederick S. and Henry T. Hopkins, "Edward Kienholz," *Art in America,* Vol. 53, October-November 1965, pp. 70-73.

Willard, Charlotte. "Violence and Art," *Art in America,* Vol. 57, January-February 1969, pp. 36-47.

Designed by Helen Kirkpatrick

Typographic Composition by
Volk and Huxley, Inc.

Printed in the United States of America
by S. D. Scott Printing Co., Inc.

Photographs by Oliver Baker; Harry Bennett;
Ferdinand Boesch; Rudolph Burckhardt;
Geoffrey Clements; Jonas Dovydenas; Frank
Lerner for Time, Inc.; Eric Pollitzer;
Nathan Rabin; Walter Rosenblum; Amalie
Rothschild; John D. Schiff; Stone and
Steccati; F. J. Thomas; John F. Waggaman.